Definitive Guide™
to
SOC-as-a-Service

The Essential Elements of
Advanced Threat Detection and Response

AF681693

Crystal Bedell
Mark Bouchard, CISSP

Foreword by Brian NeSmith

CYBEREDGE
PRESS

Definitive Guide™ to SOC-as-a-Service

Published by:
CyberEdge Group, LLC
1997 Annapolis Exchange Parkway
Suite 300
Annapolis, MD 21401
(800) 327-8711
www.cyber-edge.com

Copyright © 2018, CyberEdge Group, LLC. All rights reserved. Definitive Guide™ and the CyberEdge Press logo are trademarks of CyberEdge Group, LLC in the United States and other countries. All other trademarks and registered trademarks are the property of their respective owners.

Except as permitted under the United States Copyright Act of 1976, no part of this publication may be reproduced, stored in a retrieval system or transmitted in any form or by any means, electronic, mechanical, photocopying, recording, scanning or otherwise, without the prior written permission of the publisher. Requests to the publisher for permission should be addressed to Permissions Department, CyberEdge Group, 1997 Annapolis Exchange Parkway, Suite 300, Annapolis, MD, 21401 or transmitted via email to info@cyber-edge.com.

LIMIT OF LIABILITY/DISCLAIMER OF WARRANTY: THE PUBLISHER AND THE AUTHOR MAKE NO REPRESENTATIONS OR WARRANTIES WITH RESPECT TO THE ACCURACY OR COMPLETENESS OF THE CONTENTS OF THIS WORK AND SPECIFICALLY DISCLAIM ALL WARRANTIES, INCLUDING WITHOUT LIMITATION WARRANTIES OF FITNESS FOR A PARTICULAR PURPOSE. THE ADVICE AND STRATEGIES CONTAINED HEREIN MAY NOT BE SUITABLE FOR EVERY SITUATION. NEITHER THE PUBLISHER NOR THE AUTHOR SHALL BE LIABLE FOR DAMAGES ARISING HEREFROM. THE FACT THAT AN ORGANIZATION OR WEBSITE IS REFERRED TO IN THIS WORK AS A CITATION AND/OR A POTENTIAL SOURCE OF FURTHER INFORMATION DOES NOT MEAN THAT THE AUTHOR OR THE PUBLISHER ENDORSES THE INFORMATION THE ORGANIZATION OR WEBSITE MAY PROVIDE OR RECOMMENDATIONS IT MAY MAKE. FURTHER, READERS SHOULD BE AWARE THAT INTERNET WEBSITES LISTED IN THIS WORK MAY HAVE CHANGED OR DISAPPEARED BETWEEN WHEN THIS WORK WAS WRITTEN AND WHEN IT IS READ.

For general information on CyberEdge Group research and marketing consulting services, or to create a custom *Definitive Guide* book for your organization, contact our sales department at 800-327-8711 or info@cyber-edge.com.

ISBN: 978-0-9990354-0-5 (paperback); ISBN: 978-0-9990354-1-2 (eBook)

Printed in the United States of America.

10 9 8 7 6 5 4 3 2 1

Publisher's Acknowledgements

CyberEdge Group thanks the following individuals for their respective contributions:

Editor: Susan Shuttleworth
Designer: Debbi Stocco
Production Coordinator: Valerie Lowery
Special Help from Arctic Wolf Networks: Brian NeSmith, Narayan Makaram, Young-sae Song, David Martin, Lane Roush, Ed Jones, and Roland Goity

Table of Contents

Foreword

I don't feel safe when I'm connected to the Internet, and I never will. I'm embarrassed to admit this. Along with every new piece of technology, my industry has offered a corresponding new protection and the promise that buying it will make you safe. It's a lie. A well-crafted lie, but still a lie.

What the cybersecurity industry fails to articulate is that everyone is at risk. People, companies of all sizes, governments, schools, organizations, and even elections. Cybercriminals operate in a target-rich environment; they are out to hack anyone and everyone, not just the big companies.

If you think that technology alone will protect you from hackers, you're mistaken. At the 2016 Usenix Enigma Conference, Rob Joyce, the nation's "hacker-in-chief" and former head of the NSA's Tailored Access Operations, stated, "[With] any large network, I will tell you that persistence and focus will get you in..." What he means is that a hacker with persistence only has to be successful once, whereas the defense has to work every time.

How do you counter that? Joyce provides a solution in the context of keeping NSA spies out of the network. He considers "An out-of-band network tap"—a device that monitors network activity and produces logs that can record anomalous activity—plus a smart system administrator who actually reads the logs and pays attention to what they say, to be a nightmare for the agency. In other words, you need a security operations center (SOC).

We see this every day. One particular Arctic Wolf customer, a regional healthcare provider, had installed great perimeter security. But a crafty phishing email was able to entice not one, not two, but dozens of users to click on a link that triggered a download of malware. The Arctic Wolf SOC recognized the protection failure and informed the customer so that remediation could take place before extremely sensitive and personal information from patient health records could be extracted. Like this customer, you will inevitably experience a failure of protection, but a SOC will inform you when it does so that you can take immediate action to prevent any real damage.

That's why this guide covers all aspects of building a SOC versus buying a SOC-as-a-service. Regardless of size, every organization today needs a SOC to provide robust security. A SOC provides complete visibility into all IT infrastructure along with continuous monitoring and capabilities for threat detection and response. It's manned around the clock by security experts who can determine the true extent of incoming threats and lead the charge when it's time to address them.

Of course, there's a catch. A SOC is incredibly expensive, is time-consuming to operate, and requires at least one expert security engineer on staff. Unless you're a large corporate enterprise or aspire to be one soon, you'd better think twice before bringing a SOC in house.

That's not to say small to midsize enterprises don't have options. Managed service providers—some specializing in security—provide outsourced solutions that may address many critical security needs, including threat detection and response. The cost and range of their offerings can be vast and, just like choosing between a stay at a Motel 6 or a Four Seasons hotel, it all depends on a customer's needs and budget.

Managed security service providers have largely failed, however. They relieve their customers of the burden of managing infrastructure, but customers must still do the heavy lifting, such as daily triage, forensics and advanced analytics. That's why it often makes sense for organizations to go with a SOC-as-a-service provider, such as Arctic Wolf. We provide an affordable, subscription-based, outsourced SOC with the most advanced technology and all the security experts needed to run the show.

It's critical to fully protect your organization by implementing the most essential element of modern security. Read the Definitive Guide to SOC-as-a-Service and find the best route for your organization to benefit from a security operations center.

Brian NeSmith
Co-Founder and CEO
Arctic Wolf Networks

Introduction

Enterprise security has changed radically over the last 10 years. Antivirus and spam filters no longer provide adequate protection. Attackers bypass preventive controls and access networks for weeks, sometimes months, before they're caught—*if* they get caught. No company is safe.

Large enterprises build security operations centers (SOCs) to stop these advanced threats, but smaller companies lack the resources. To continue to compete in the cyberworld, small and medium enterprises must have equal access to advanced security capabilities. As a smaller enterprise, your organization needs the ability to:

- Detect and respond to advanced security threats in real time
- Leverage the expertise of an experienced security staff to improve your overall security posture
- Work with skilled security engineers who understand your IT environment and business risks
- Reduce the cost of protecting your IT environment
- Focus on the business, knowing a trusted provider has your back

This book explores how any company can take advantage of a SOC-as-a-service to obtain the security capabilities and outcomes that until recently were only accessible to large enterprises.

Chapters at a Glance

Chapter 1, "Cyberthreats—The Great Equalizer," examines how cyberthreats have evolved, and their impact on small and medium enterprises.

Chapter 2, "Why Point Products Are Not Enough," explains the role of point products in a modern security strategy, as well as the challenges they present.

Chapter 3, "Why a SIEM Solution Is Not Sufficient," describes SIEM solutions and their capabilities, and why they have a high failure rate.

Chapter 4, "Understanding the Security Operations Center," explains what a SOC is and the technology, people, and processes that comprise one.

Chapter 5, "SOC Options—Getting What You Need," reviews the three options for obtaining SOC capabilities.

Chapter 6, "The Role of Managed Services," introduces the capabilities of various managed services providers, including managed detection and response.

Chapter 7, "A Closer Look at SOC-as-a-Service," explores the inner workings of SOCaaS and how it complements managed services.

Chapter 8, "Top 10 Next-gen SOCaaS Capabilities," enumerates criteria for choosing a SOCaaS provider.

The Glossary provides handy definitions of key terms (appearing in *italics*) used throughout this book.

Helpful Icons

TIP

Tips provide practical advice that you can apply in your own organization.

DON'T FORGET

When you see this icon, take note as the related content contains key information that you won't want to forget.

CAUTION

Proceed with caution because if you don't it may prove costly to you and your organization.

TECH TALK

Content associated with this icon is more technical in nature and is intended for IT practitioners.

ON THE WEB

Want to learn more? Follow the corresponding URL to discover additional content available on the Web.

Chapter 1

Cyberthreats— The Great Equalizer

In this chapter

- Learn why and how cyberthreats have evolved
- Understand common tactics cyberattackers use today
- Explore current trends in security delivery models

It wasn't long ago that cyberattacks were primarily the concern of large enterprises. They had the digital assets worthy of targeting, as well as the resources needed to protect them.

Ten years ago, IT security professionals at small to midsize enterprises (SMEs) mostly worried about *mass attacks*. They considered themselves adequately covered with antivirus and firewall software. After all, what more could they suffer beyond a virus attack or website defacement?

This chapter discusses how the evolution of cyberthreats has changed the way small and medium enterprises must think about their security strategy.

Cyberthreats Have Evolved

Nothing stands still in the world of technology. As consumers, we know this well—every six months brings a new gadget or two to replace those acquired just a short time before. A similar evolution is taking place in the world of cyberattacks.

Attacks are growing more sophisticated

The mass attacks observed in the early days of the Internet caused their fair share of disruption—which is exactly what they were designed to do. Attackers were opportunistic. They exploited unpatched vulnerabilities and developed malware (malicious software) with the primary intent of wreaking havoc.

The goal of a mass attack was to draw attention to the perpetrator and earn notoriety among the hacker community. A virus infection that was part of a mass attack could just as easily impact an SME as a large enterprise. As far as attackers were concerned, *who* was attacked didn't matter as much as *how many* were attacked.

Much has changed since then. The mass attacks that were popular 10 years ago are largely unsuccessful today. Perimeter-based controls like firewalls and web filters stop unwanted traffic from entering the network. Prevention-based tools such as antivirus software identify and block known malware and viruses. But the war against cyberthreats is far from over.

While security providers honed their perimeter prevention tools to use signature-based controls, attackers evolved their tactics, techniques, and procedures to bypass such controls with malware obfuscation methods.

TECH TALK

Most perimeter and prevention tools are *signature based.* They identify attacks based on patterns in the code. But these tools can only detect threats that have already been identified. That means someone, somewhere, must fall victim to an attack before it can be detected.

One of the ways attackers bypass signature-based tools is by leveraging a *zero-day threat,* which exploits an unknown vulnerability. Because there is no fix or patch for the vulnerability, and the threat itself is also unknown, the attack can bypass perimeter or preventive controls and enter a private network undetected. This is key because the attacker's motive is no longer to draw attention to himself.

Attackers today are driven by something more tangible than celebrity status. They're motivated by financial gain. The longer they can remain undetected on the enterprise network, the longer they can exfiltrate valuable corporate assets, whether they're sensitive customer data, intellectual property, or everyday operational files.

The bottom line is that these assets have financial value. Attackers can sell intellectual property on the dark web or use sensitive customer data to commit financial fraud. Even operational files have value.

CAUTION

Attackers today use a variety of tactics:

- *Ransomware* is a type of malicious software that encrypts the user's files or data, rendering them illegible until the user pays a ransom. Attackers might up the ante by threatening to delete all data or release it to the public if the victim attempts to decrypt the data on their own—or chooses not to pay the ransom.
- A *phishing attack* leverages *social engineering* to lure victims into divulging personal or sensitive information. Attackers pose as a trusted organization and request, often by email, that the recipient visit a web page to update their personal information. The email itself and the web page mimic the branding of the legitimate company. This deception helps persuade the victim to submit information that is acquired by the attacker, including user credentials.
- A *brute-force attack* uses a systematic process to uncover a user's account password or PIN. Automated software continuously generates possible passwords or PINs until the right combination is submitted and the attacker obtains access.
- Cyberthreats aren't always lurking in the dark web. Sometimes they're the result of the organization's own negligence. *Departed user access* occurs when employees or contractors leave the company and their accounts are not properly deprovisioned. Users can continue to access corporate resources when they have no legitimate reason for doing so. They can use this access to obtain data and files, often without drawing the attention of the IT department.

No organization is safe

CAUTION

Attackers can cash in big by invading large enterprises, but they don't have to. SMEs also have valuable data and are often easier pickings. Because they have a weaker security posture, once inside the network, attackers can stay hidden longer.

Limited IT budget

The No. 1 challenge small and medium enterprises face when it comes to shoring up their defenses is a limited IT budget. They simply lack the financial resources needed to properly operate their network, let alone hunt down security threats in their environment.

Security skills shortage

The IT industry as a whole is suffering from a severe cyber security skills shortage. This is due, in part, to the growing complexity of today's IT environments. The morphing network topology requires new, more-dynamic defense tools and strategies. Staying abreast of the skillsets needed while responding to rising business demands requires one technology we haven't mastered: human cloning.

Meanwhile, small and medium organizations simply can't compete with larger enterprises for talent due to their aforementioned budget issues. The job market for security professionals is heavily in large organizations' favor, as they have the budget to offer competitive salaries that are difficult for smaller organizations to match.

Growing attack surface

It wasn't so long ago that protecting user endpoints meant installing antivirus on company-provisioned laptops and desktops. Today, those endpoints represent a small portion of the IT environment, as end users bring their personally owned smartphones and tablet computers to work and sign up for cloud-based business applications. As Figure 1-1 shows, each new mobile device, Internet of Things connection (with medical devices, smart TVs, etc.), and cloud-based application introduced into the corporate network increases the attack surface exponentially.

Solving the problem is not just a matter of applying additional preventive controls and technology. It also requires continuously monitoring these assets to ensure they are protected against new threats, and regularly patching them to fix known vulnerabilities.

One way to put the problem in perspective is to consider the different flavors and versions of operating systems that need to be tracked and patched on these devices. Prior to the advent of the smartphone, many corporations were purely Microsoft shops. There was no need to worry about Apple iOS- and Android-related threats because those operating systems didn't exist in the environment. But that all changed when users started bringing their iOS and Android devices to the office, providing attackers with a new way into the network.

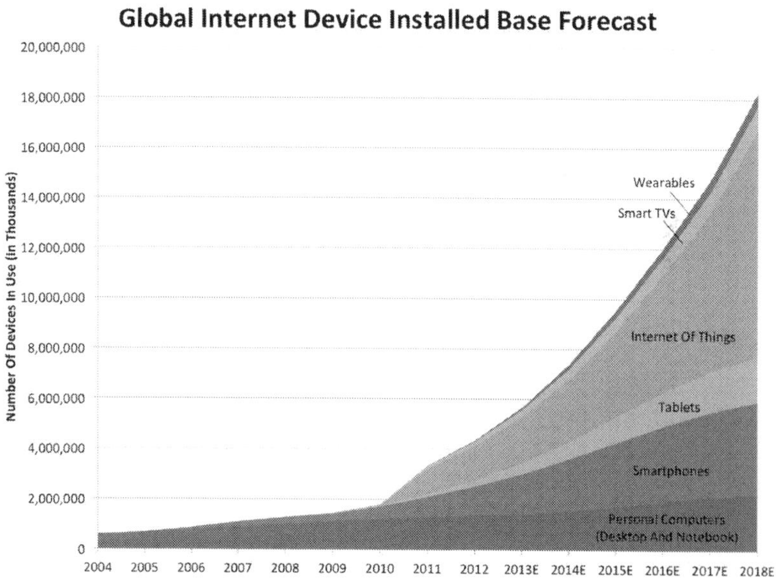

Figure 1-1: The number of devices connected to the Internet is increasing exponentially. (BI Intelligence)

Fortunately, Security Has Evolved, Too

The security industry doesn't operate in a vacuum. Technology providers are also evolving their offerings to keep pace with attackers and make their solutions more accessible to SMEs.

Delivery models make security capabilities more accessible

There was a time when procuring a security service or technology introduced significant overhead. The IT organization could never just buy a payroll application, for example. It was a given that the new application required servers to run on and other hardware for data storage, all of which had to be maintained and managed.

TIP

Fortunately, there are other delivery models available today that reduce your organization's overhead and the overall costs involved in the product's procurement.

Managed Security Services

Managed security service providers (MSSPs) offer specific security capabilities on a subscription basis. Their primary focus is remote device management. For example, MSSPs will configure and maintain your firewalls and intrusion detection and prevention systems over the network. You still keep your hardware on premises, but you essentially outsource the personnel (and expertise) required to manage them. This approach helps reduce the operational burden associated with maintaining your security tools.

Cloud-enabled security-as-a-service

Hiring IT staff and purchasing and installing a trouble-ticketing system to deliver these services on premises is expensive. Similarly, buying security technologies and hiring skilled workers to manage these complex technologies is expensive and time consuming.

Security-as-a-service (SecaaS) provides security services in the cloud. Examples include cloud access security brokerage (CASB) such as Netskope, identity-as-a-service (IDaaS) such as Okta and Centrify, and security operations center-as-a-service (SOCaaS), which we'll discuss further in Chapter 7.

SecaaS solutions significantly reduce the costs associated with deploying a new security solution. They require little or no capital outlay and significantly reduce operational expenses associated with the solution. The application itself is maintained and managed offsite by the provider. There may be some administration required for setup, but it's limited compared to a traditional software solution.

SecaaS customers also benefit from scalability. SecaaS solutions can scale up or down on demand. Customers typically pay only for what they use—without any need for additional setup. In addition, customers benefit from ongoing software fixes and updates, which means they get access to new capabilities (read: improved security) more often than they do with software that runs on premises.

Shifting focus

All of these trends in security—the growing sophistication of cyberattacks, the increased risk to SMEs, the availability of additional delivery models—have, in turn, forced IT organizations to shift their attention. Instead of focusing their resources on prevention controls—which have proven largely ineffective against *advanced persistent threats*—large enterprises have shifted their investments to focus on detection and response capabilities, as illustrated in Figure 1-2.

DON'T FORGET

Prevention tools continue to play a valuable role in protecting an enterprise, but they are not the be-all and end-all. Without investments in detection and response capabilities, organizations don't have what it takes to detect advanced persistent threats in a timely manner—or at all. They cannot monitor the IT environment continuously, detect and analyze anomalous activity, contain and mitigate an attack, etc.

Bolstering your organization's detection and response capabilities is a challenge because these functions are not available as technology. They require skilled personnel, which—as we already explained—are in high demand and short supply.

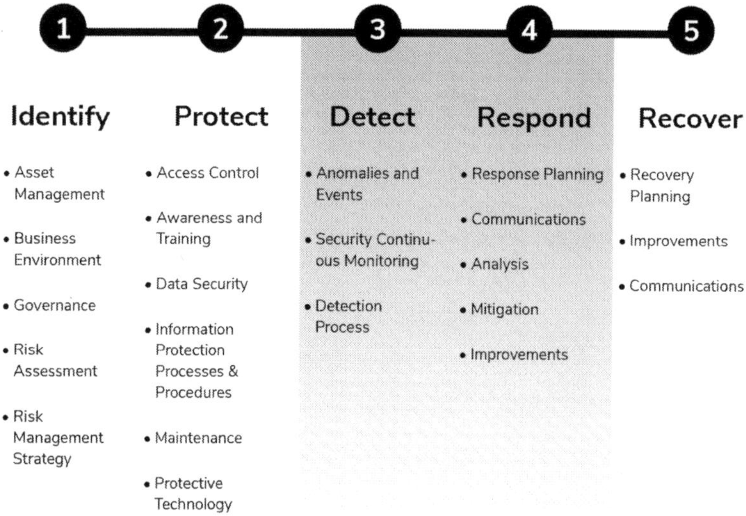

Figure 1-2: The NIST Cybersecurity Framework defines five phases of the cyber security management lifecycle.

Trends in Incident Response

According to the 2017 Cost of Data Breach Study by the Ponemon Institute:

- "The time to identify and contain data breaches impacts costs."
- For criminal and malicious attacks, the average time for an organization to identify an attack was 214 days. The average time to contain an attack was 77 days.
- "Having tools that heighten detective or forensic capabilities can significantly reduce data breach cost."

Chapter 2

Why Point Products Are Not Enough

In this chapter

- Learn what a point product is
- Examine the three main categories of security point products
- Understand the limitations of point products

Layered security is a best practice for protecting digital assets. The concept, called *defense-in-depth*, is borrowed from military strategy. The strategy involves implementing different defense mechanisms at different layers throughout the IT environment so that if one mechanism fails, the next might stop an attack from progressing further.

DON'T FORGET

A layered approach to security isn't just beneficial, it's a requirement for today's IT environments and their loosely defined network perimeters. The increasing use of mobile devices and cloud-based applications (SaaS) has dissolved the network perimeter, giving users and attackers multiple points of access into the corporate IT environment. Each of these access points requires its own defense mechanisms, including point products, as part of a defense-in-depth strategy.

Limitations of Point Products

A *point product* is designed to solve a specific problem. Anti-malware software, for example, is intended to protect your systems from becoming infected by malicious software. It does not, however, stop an attacker from sending a flood of network traffic to your website in a denial-of-service attack. You need protection against both types of attacks—as well as myriad others. Each new type of attack or technology added to the network creates a need for a new point product—or two, or three.

There are three categories of point products that companies deploy as part of a defense-in-depth strategy.

Network security

Network security solutions focus on—you guessed it—the network. This category of solutions includes firewalls, web filters, and intrusion prevention and detection solutions. They are designed to stop malicious traffic from entering or exiting the network.

Network security vendors have evolved their products to better protect networks against advanced threats. A modern next-generation firewall offers all the capabilities you find in a traditional firewall: basic packet filtering, network and port address translation, and stateful packet inspection. But it also provides threat detection capabilities based on traffic behavioral analysis, threat signatures, and anomalous activity.

Network security solutions can also show you what is happening on the network. For example, they can be great at detecting malware moving laterally across the network. Unfortunately, they don't provide full visibility into your endpoints.

CAUTION

Network security solutions are known for generating a lot of false positives. You may receive an alert because malware is on the network, but your endpoints may have already been patched.

Endpoint security

Traditional endpoint protection (EPP) solutions provide necessary but limited protection of end-user computing devices—laptops, desktops, and mobile devices.

EPP solutions encompass a variety of prevention technologies, including anti-malware, personal firewall, vulnerability assessment, application whitelisting, and enterprise mobility management. However, as signature- and policy-based technologies, they can reliably identify and block only known threats.

Endpoint detection and response (EDR) is a more advanced category of endpoint security solutions. They're designed to detect anomalous activity on endpoints, and therefore have a better chance of detecting unknown malware strains in zero-day attacks.

However, EDR systems rarely take action in real time. Typically, telemetry is sent to a central management system, which performs analysis and correlation, and then fires an alert. Analysts must then review the alerts to figure out if there's really a threat present—or if it's just a false alarm. The complexity of EDR technologies necessitates security staff trained in endpoint detection and response.

EPP and EDR typically require an agent to run on the endpoint, and neither solution provides full network visibility. If, for example, a database password is compromised, an EDR will not stop an attacker from logging in remotely and exfiltrating sensitive data. Application layer attacks, like SQL injections, zero-day vulnerabilities, and other forms of web-based attacks, are also beyond the scope of an EDR.

Data security

Endpoints and networks are simply means to an end. Attackers use them as a way of entering the IT environment so they can get what they're really after: business-critical data.

Companies that operate in highly regulated industries or firms that are extra cautious about data security may deploy data and application security products. Because of their cost, these solutions are usually deployed only on critical assets. The solutions also introduce performance overhead, as every database request is inspected to ensure that the data is not being exfiltrated by a malicious user or script.

Figure 2-1 illustrates the three categories of point solutions commonly deployed as part of a defense-in-depth strategy.

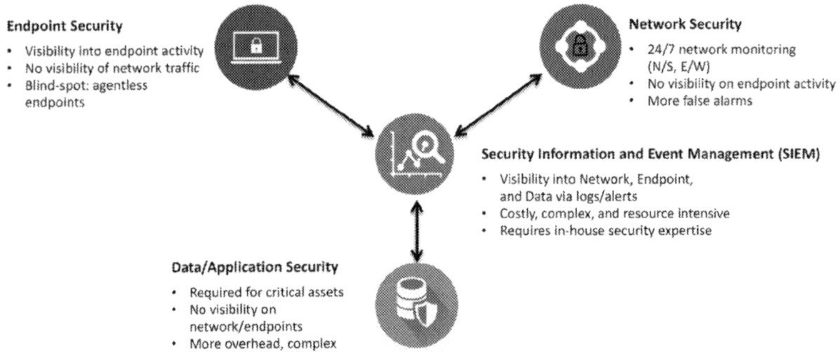

Figure 2-1: Three types of point solutions and their limitations.

Where They Fall Short

Point products play an important role in protecting your company's digital assets, but gaps still remain, making it difficult for security teams to detect and stop attacks as they move through the environment. The problem is three-fold:

- ☑ No comprehensive visibility. Teams need 360-degree visibility across endpoint, data, and network security tools to understand what's happening in the environment.
- ☑ No correlation across products. Teams need to understand how the alerts generated by a single point product relate to those by another so that they can get to the root of the problem.
- ☑ No contextual intelligence in alerts for response actions. Alerts indicate that something has gone wrong in the environment—a threshold has been met, for example—but give no indication of how to fix it or prevent it from happening again.

Chapter 3

Why a SIEM Solution Is Not Sufficient

In this chapter

- Find out what a SIEM solution is
- Explore what a SIEM solution can do for you
- Understand why organizations have a high failure rate with SIEM solutions

Security practitioners face the overwhelming task of making sense of a barrage of alerts coming from myriad point products. This is nearly impossible to do without 360-degree visibility across the environment, automated event correlation, and contextual evidence. To get holistic visibility, you need the log aggregation and correlation capabilities provided by a *security information and event management solution*—SIEM, for short.

What's a SIEM?

TECH TALK

A SIEM solution is a software system comprised of two technologies: a SIM and a SEM. A security information management system (SIM) provides log management capabilities, such as real-time log monitoring and analysis. A security events management system (SEM) serves as a correlation engine. When the SIM and SEM systems work together as a SIEM solution, they provide the visibility, event correlation, and contextual evidence organizations need to begin making sense of their security alerts.

SIEM capabilities

SIEMs are typically deployed by large enterprises that have the budget and personnel to implement and manage advanced technologies. However, midsize organizations are increasingly considering SIEMs as well because they too can benefit from the critical capabilities these solutions claim to deliver:

- ☑ Comprehensive visibility: A SIEM solution aggregates the log records of every endpoint and network device, and provides visibility into system and network activity through a single pane of glass. It also provides a complete record of every event that happens in the environment.
- ☑ Detection of threats, and unusual user and device activity: By correlating log data from various point solutions, a SIEM solution can help security teams piece together clues and identify anomalous activity that may indicate a threat.
- ☑ More effective analytics: A SIEM solution can provide security teams with pertinent information that helps prioritize and address specific alerts. Because every event is logged, teams know an intrusion's origin, where it's spread, and the best way to respond to it.
- ☑ Streamlined compliance reporting: Having all log data in one place—the SIEM solution—simplifies compliance reporting.

A SIEM Tool Is Just the Start

CAUTION

Any company stands to benefit from the capabilities we just described. The tricky part is overcoming the challenges that a SIEM solution introduces. Unfortunately, the above capabilities come at a hefty cost that goes well beyond the initial capital outlay.

To operate effectively and successfully detect cyberattacks, a SIEM solution must be well architected and implemented, and continuously tuned. These are not easy tasks. Success relies on the skillsets of those who continuously manage the SIEM, as well as the best practices used to respond to incidents.

Risky business

As any IT or security practitioner will tell you, no technology is a panacea. However, a SIEM solution has more than its fair share of risks and downsides. As we look at what those are, you'll begin to understand why organizations have a high failure rate with SIEMs.

Complexity

CAUTION

There's nothing simple about a SIEM solution. But that shouldn't come as a complete surprise. We're talking about a system that takes in data from a number of disparate sources and attempts to make something out of it. The problems associated with a SIEM are that it requires security experts to continuously leverage the information to identify real incidents, and a full-time development team to keep the information updated and correlated for the security experts' workflow. Without these two human resources, a SIEM is an expensive log data storage system.

Deployment

You might think that deploying a SIEM is simple. You just connect the SIEM to raw log sources, right? Yes... and no.

A SIEM solution works best when it's connected to the right information sources. A security engineer should identify all of the security devices, end-user laptops/desktops, Internet of Things devices, and business-critical servers, databases, and applications from which log data will be collected. The business-critical network segments to be monitored must also be identified.

From here, deployment becomes increasingly challenging. A SIEM solution can ingest raw syslog records, but the correlations rules engine can't analyze them. You must therefore build parsers to convert raw log data into structured data that can be filtered based on fields. But this process isn't foolproof. Data is commonly miscategorized by the SIEM—and those instances must be fixed.

TIP

When all is said and done, SIEM deployment cycles can run anywhere from six to 12 months. During this time, you aren't seeing any value from your investment, and your staff's attention is focused on deploying a tool—not securing the IT environment. Once a SIEM has been deployed and tuned, it's ready for action and the real work starts.

Administration

A SIEM's rules require constant tuning. Security engineers and developers must continually build and refine correlation rules, and must subscribe to the latest threat intelligence feeds to accurately identify the latest attack vectors.

Every time your device and endpoint software vendors issue patches and updates, you must also update the SIEM parsers for these devices. If the parser doesn't match the supported version, you risk getting thousands of false positives.

Ongoing administration and operation generally require multiple security operators, security analysts, and incident responders.

Operations

Unfortunately, a SIEM solution doesn't completely solve the problems associated with point solutions that we discussed in Chapter 2. In fact, according to a survey by the Ponemon Institute, 70% of respondents said current SIEM technologies do not provide the most accurate, prioritized, and meaningful alerts.

DON'T FORGET

A SIEM solution can reduce the noise generated by point solutions if it's continuously managed properly. In fact, a SIEM solution can generate thousands of alerts per day, many of which may be false positives. To efficiently process the output, a SIEM solution requires 24x7 monitoring and response. Security engineers must make sense of a SIEM's output to fine-tune the correlation rules and determine which alerts require further investigation or immediate attention. Manual or automated workflows must be in place to act on the output accordingly.

Cost

CAUTION

Like complexity, the costs of a SIEM solution manifest themselves in a number of ways. Here are some of the many factors you need to consider when budgeting for a SIEM solution.

Resources

All that complexity we just talked about? It adds up in the form of operational costs. In fact, experts estimate that for every dollar spent on a SIEM tool, companies spend three dollars to manage it.

Let's put this into perspective: on average, it takes a security analyst about an hour to acknowledge and act on eight to 10 security events. An organization with 200 users may produce an average of 100 critical alerts per day. That's enough to completely occupy two full-time security experts. And you still need someone to update and manage the SIEM system, agents, reports, and security integrations.

The more complex your IT environment, the more resources you'll need to manage a SIEM solution. If your IT environment is like most these days and consists of a mix of internally and externally hosted services or the use of SaaS, you can count on multiplying the number of staff needed to manage a SIEM tool.

Data volume, velocity, and variety

TIP

The volume, velocity, and variety of data generated by the IT environment are increasing rapidly. This is a benefit for today's IT organizations, as SIEM solutions perform best when they can access multiple high-volume data sources in real time. The more data you have, the more detailed a picture you get of the activity taking place in your IT environment.

But the growing volume, velocity, and variety of data also benefit SIEM *providers*, who charge customers using consumption- or volume-based pricing models. Customers are billed according to the number of devices from which log data is consumed, or the volume/velocity of log data as measured in events per second. As a result, customers can experience unpredictable cost increases.

This puts organizations between a rock and a hard place as they are forced to choose between protection and visibility or sticking to their budget. When budget wins, customers end up with incomplete data and blind spots in the environment.

Over-engineered systems

It's normal for the amount of log data generated by the IT environment to fluctuate. It can increase or decrease based on the time of day or year. During an incident or attack, the volume of data increases—by as much as two to three times the ordinary volume.

Your SIEM system must be designed to handle these data spikes. As a result, SIEM providers over-engineer their systems to handle at least twice the ordinary workload. This ensures that the system doesn't fail during an attack. But it also means that you pay for the level of security your company requires on its worst day, every day.

Unpredictability

The IT environment is anything but fixed. On any given day, devices and systems are upgraded, new ones are added, and patches are deployed. Meanwhile, the number of logs and volume of collected data increase. A SIEM provider's cost estimate is therefore just that: an estimate. This variability makes budget planning incredibly challenging, and the bottom line much higher than originally estimated.

Performance

CAUTION

In an ideal world, a SIEM solution would operate in near- real time all of the time. The truth of the matter is that underperformance is typically the norm for SIEM solutions.

Multi-tasking

A SIEM solution is tasked with a lot: log data ingestion, correlation, analysis, searching, and reporting. To get it all done, providers design their solutions to multi-task. But a majority of SIEM vendors use one engine to do it all. This causes the functions to interfere with one another. Running a search, for example, will pause collection and other non-critical functions.

Forklift upgrades

SIEM vendors often sell different classes of hardware, each of which ingests, parses, and analyzes/correlates a certain amount of log data. Eventually you will reach the maximum capacity of your initial platform, essentially outgrowing the hardware. When this happens, you have no choice but to upgrade to the next-higher-capacity platform. This upgrade can double or even triple the cost of the original SIEM solution.

Reporting delays

Detecting anomalies and threats is a critical SIEM function. Reporting is not. So, while a SIEM solution is designed to analyze log data in real time, reporting performance leaves something to be desired.

Furthermore, a SIEM solution typically only reports on just one or two weeks of data. If you want to report on more data, you'll need additional products. Quarterly reporting necessitates dedicated log management tools, while multi-year reporting requires a more significant investment, such as a big data security analytics product.

Input vs. output

Feeding a SIEM only a few data sources reduces its detection efficacy. In addition, out-of-the-box correlation is very limited, thereby requiring commitment of operators or analysts to write and maintain extensive sets of correlation rules.

False positives

Finally, a SIEM solution is very susceptible to false positives. Because it's so carefully calibrated, the smallest change in agent configuration or log sources can result in a large volume of false positives.

DIY: At Least 3 Times More Expensive Than the Cost of SIEM

Think twice before you embark on the do-it-yourself journey of managing your own SIEM. Apart from the licensing cost of the SIEM platform and additional processing power and storage needed to consume your peak volume of log data, you will have to hire a skilled team of security experts to manage it 24x7, and subscribe to multiple threat intelligence services to enable you to accurately detect the latest attack vectors.

In fact, experts estimate that for every dollar spent on a SIEM tool, companies spend three dollars to manage it.

Filling in the Gaps

With enough time and money, many of the SIEM challenges we described can be overcome. But most SME organizations today are running on shoestring budgets, and even if they aren't, they'd rather invest in the business than in shoring up a SIEM solution.

What's more, a fully working and optimized SIEM solution may still fail to combat new attacks. Don't get us wrong—a SIEM tool plays a valuable role in today's security programs. But it's just one piece of a bigger solution. The sophisticated nature of today's evolving attacks requires that you supplement your SIEM tool with people and processes in what's known as a *security operations center*.

Chapter 4

Understanding the Security Operations Center

In this chapter

- Understand the capabilities provided by a security operations center (SOC)
- Review the difference between a network operations center and a SOC
- Explore the technology, people, and processes that comprise a SOC

As a technology, a SIEM solution can do a lot. It can help your IT organization understand what's happening in the environment. It can collect the alerts generated by your network security, data security, and endpoint products. It can dedupe those alerts and show you how an attack is progressing through the environment. However, you need security experts with the right skills and knowledge of forensics analysis and incident response processes to help you make sense of critical incidents that need immediate attention. A SIEM is the core tool/technology needed for a SOC to function. However, there are a lot more systems, processes, and people that go into building out a SOC–and it gets more difficult as the IT environment grows.

CAUTION

Over the years, IT organizations have seen exponential increases in the volume of log data pouring into their SIEMs. These increases have the adverse effect of generating considerable "noise." In other words, security professionals have to filter through more events and alerts to identify and prioritize incidents that pose a real business risk. Furthermore, to detect advanced persistent threats, security professionals must monitor a SIEM 24x7.

Beyond personnel who manage and operate the SIEM itself, organizations require processes that enable real-time response to threats, security professionals who can perform forensics analysis, and managers who can oversee these efforts and fine-tune them to ensure efficiency. In short, IT organizations need a security operations center.

Welcome to the SOC

DON'T FORGET

A *security operations center* (SOC) is a centralized unit comprised of skilled people, processes, and technologies working together to deliver end-to-end security capabilities. These include the prevention, detection, and investigation of, and response to, cybersecurity threats and incidents.

A SOC is analogous to an air traffic control center, focusing on security activities instead of flight operations. The SOC provides centralized visibility of all the activity occurring in your environment. Instead of managing planes that are landing, taking off, and taxiing to the gates, the SOC provides visibility into who is logging into your systems, what devices are connected to the network, what data is being accessed, what threats are present, the health of security devices, and more. Also, like air traffic controllers, skilled people are watching all of this activity, 24 hours a day, seven days a week, in an effort to identify and remediate problems before they impact the business.

A SOC is the most essential element of a modern security strategy, as it provides the only means to detect, contain, and remediate advanced threats. A SOC is the next step in the evolution of security. It also serves as the foundation for containment and remediation—key capabilities for mitigating advanced persistent threats.

As with SIEM systems, there was a time when only the largest enterprises had a SOC. That situation has changed because businesses of all sizes, including SMEs, need a SOC to help combat advanced persistent threats. A SOC can help SMEs close the gap (as shown in Figure 4-1) that exists between where they are today and where they want to be.

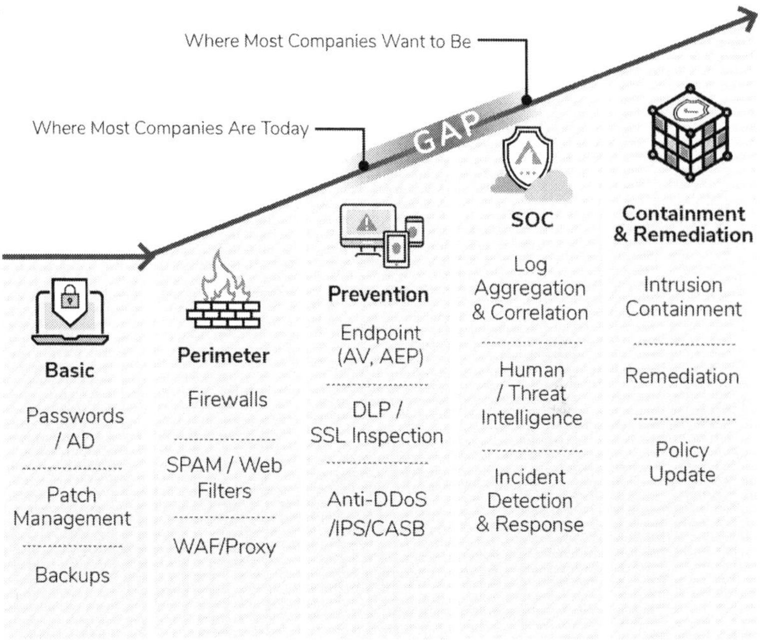

Figure 4-1: By delivering advanced security capabilities, a SOC enables IT organizations to achieve a mature security posture.

TECH TALK

A SOC provides the following capabilities:

- ☑ Real-time threat detection and response. The SOC staff determines the best method or technologies for threat detection and response. The SOC itself includes all of the human and machine intelligence needed to collect and analyze machine data in real time, detect threats, and remediate them.
- ☑ 24x7 monitoring of system log data and network traffic. Continuous monitoring ensures that anomalous and malicious activity from either outsiders or insiders is detected in real time. Staff identifies malicious activity as it occurs, enabling teams to respond immediately and help eliminate—or at least reduce—its damage.

- ☑ A comprehensive and centralized view of a company's security posture. A SOC integrates the data coming from your tools to provide a snapshot of your current security posture.
- ☑ Threat hunting and investigation. The SOC staff proactively searches through your networks and data to identify threats that have evaded your perimeter controls and are hiding, undetected, on the network.

But I Already Have a NOC

It's important to understand that a *network operations center* (NOC) is not a SOC. A NOC is a centralized unit that's focused on monitoring and managing the enterprise network and the devices on it. A NOC is typically staffed with IT personnel whose tasks include managing data backups, ensuring network availability and performance, and rolling out patches. IT folks have plenty to contend with without also being held responsible for maintaining security. Even if they did have the time, IT staff rarely have the appropriate skillsets to take on security duties.

Bottom line: Your NOC is NOT a SOC. Don't treat it as one.

Equipping a SOC: Technology

A SOC is comprised of a diverse range of advanced tools that monitor the security of an organization's systems and network infrastructure. The core technology used in a SOC is a SIEM solution. As we described in Chapter 3, a SIEM solution collects and correlates log data and network flows from sensors placed throughout the network.

A SIEM solution provides a complete record of everything that happens in the IT environment, enabling security engineers to identify indicators of compromise, malware intrusion, and other unusual network activity. Because every event is logged, security engineers have the visibility they need to identify the origin of an intrusion, track (or see) where it has spread, and determine the best response.

TECH TALK

Other technologies found in a SOC:

- ☑ **Intrusion detection tools** analyze traffic and perform packet logging on IP networks. They are used to monitor networks or systems and identify malicious activity or policy violations.
- ☑ **Workflow tools** provide some level of automation and help keep everyone focused on the proper task. To be effective, workflow tools require repeatable processes, which we'll discuss later in this chapter.
- ☑ **Application programming interfaces (APIs)** enable systems and software to communicate. APIs are used in a SOC to connect cloud-based resources to the SIEM.
- ☑ **Threat intelligence feeds** provide real-time information about potential and current threats. A SOC leverages multiple threat intelligence feeds to ensure the staff has the threat indicators to detect the latest attacks happening locally and globally.
- ☑ **Reporting tools** enable the SOC team to communicate the status of the IT environment to others within the business.

Staffing a SOC: People

Of course, no technology operates itself. That's where people come in. They bring the technical skills and expertise necessary to realize the benefits of your technical investments. A SOC, therefore, is also comprised of a dedicated team of security experts and usually a team of developers.

A SOC must be staffed with a variety of people who have extensive training and experience, including formal security training and certification. Members of the SOC team also need on-the-job experience so that they are familiar with the IT environment and understand the company's business risks. Vendor-specific training is necessary so that SOC staff know how to configure and manage the various security technologies they're using.

DON'T FORGET

Roles and responsibilities for members of a SOC team may differ from one organization to another, depending on how they're assigned. However, a SOC typically consists of the following positions:

- **Security operators** help oversee SOC operations. They serve as the focal point for managing and coordinating a response to incidents.
- **Security analysts** are typically on the front lines of the SOC. They are the first to review alerts and determine their relevance and urgency. They are also responsible for investigating threats and determining appropriate steps for remediation.
- **Security researchers** study new strains of malware, take them apart, determine how they work, and share that information with others. They might also use the information they glean to better understand cyberattackers and their attack methods and behavior profiles.
- **Security managers** supervise the SOC team and handle higher-level tasks, like running reports, managing the escalation process, and reviewing incident reports. Managers also monitor the SOC's performance and communicate with business leaders.
- **An incident response team** consists of a manager, security analysts, and security researchers. The team is responsible for analyzing and responding to security breaches in an effort to minimize the impact to the business.
- **A forensics team** investigates breaches to determine root cause and, ideally, preserve evidence so that it can be used in a court of law. The team must practice proper planning, documentation, chain of custody, and rules of evidence.
- **A compliance audit team** performs periodic, comprehensive reviews of the IT environment to validate the organization's compliance with regulatory requirements. The team also performs risk assessments, understands applicable laws and regulations, monitors compliance efforts, and educates staff on audit findings.

- **A development team** maintains log source connections, API integrations, parsers, custom workflow tools, etc. A SOC leverages a development lifecycle against its platform, similar to the development process used to write software.

Operationalizing a SOC: Processes

To ensure that the SOC operates efficiently and addresses threats promptly, an organization must have strategic security processes in place.

CAUTION

A SOC must implement the following processes:

- **Security training** processes ensure that training is ongoing and comprehensive, rather than an ad hoc effort. Security personnel need regular professional certifications and vendor training to ensure that their skills stay current. They must be trained on the technologies deployed in the IT environment and SOC, as well as on advances in cyberthreats.

  Training processes help ensure that staff members are able to effectively carry out their roles and responsibilities at all times.
- **Threat hunting and investigation** processes are critical for ensuring that threat hunting and investigation efforts are consistent and repeatable. Where possible, repeatable steps should be automated.
- **Trouble ticketing** processes address how trouble tickets are escalated and tracked. The processes can and should be automated. Otherwise, the task of taking care of tickets manually can be a full-time job in a large SOC.
- **Incident response** processes ensure that the incident response team identifies, investigates, and responds to incidents in a timely manner that minimizes their impact and facilitates a rapid recovery. The processes should be repeatable and carried out consistently.
- **Threat intelligence** feeds are used properly to build correlation rules to help detect threats more accurately and reduce false positives.

Putting It All in Perspective

CAUTION

As you can see, SOCs help address some of the problems associated with SIEMs. However, SOCs are still expensive and complicated. Building one yourself is no trivial task. In the next chapter, we'll take a look at options for procuring SOC capabilities, from building your own, to co-managing a SOC, to outsourcing the whole kit and caboodle.

Chapter 5

SOC Options—Getting What You Need

In this chapter

- Explore the implications of building your own SOC
- Understand how a co-managed SOC operates
- Learn how to obtain SOC capabilities without added operational overhead

There are several available options for obtaining a security operations center (SOC). Each has pros and cons, which we explain here. As you learn about each of these, consider your organization's use case, risk tolerance, and available resources. These factors all come into play when choosing a SOC.

The three SOC models presented in this chapter are analogous to different cycling scenarios. Running a self-managed SOC is like riding a bike by yourself. A co-managed SIEM solution, where you share responsibility with a service provider, can be compared to operating a tandem bicycle with a companion. And the last option, the managed SOC, involves delegating control to a service provider, which is like riding in a bicycle trailer.

Own It All: The Self-managed SOC

The first option for obtaining SOC services is to build your own. A self-managed SOC is run by a dedicated team in a dedicated facility, located on premises.

CAUTION

Building a SOC means purchasing and deploying a SIEM solution and other technologies, hiring the appropriate personnel to manage and run them, and implementing the myriad processes we outlined in Chapter 4. As you can imagine, building and managing a SOC is not for the faint-hearted and is very expensive.

The pros and cons of a self-managed SOC

If you think managing a SIEM solution is difficult, you won't like what you're about to read. Building a SOC is even more complex, more time-consuming, and costlier than managing a SIEM solution. It can cost millions of dollars to build a SOC, making it a viable option for only the largest enterprises. Because of the effort and resources involved, most organizations consider alternatives. Even some large organizations choose to forgo the build-it-yourself option.

CAUTION

It takes a serious commitment to realize the full value of a SOC. As with a SIEM solution, you can't "set it and forget it." A SOC requires ongoing investments, and it can take years to establish a baseline level of maturity.

Staffing is arguably the most challenging aspect of building a self-managed SOC. Threat detection and response require security experts with knowledge of the latest attack vectors, access to global threat intelligence, and in-depth knowledge of your IT infrastructure. The demand for security experts outstrips the supply, and the challenge of retaining these security professionals in the current hot job market can make it difficult to build a mature knowledge base. Regardless, the professionals you hire will need regular training to stay current on threat techniques and technologies.

There are a few scenarios where building and managing your own SOC might make sense. For instance, some companies can't or don't want to outsource their SOC to a service provider. Perhaps they have a complex use case or regulatory compliance requirements that make outsourcing difficult. For example, organizational policies at the Department of Defense do not allow outsourcing.

However, most analysts and security experts advise SME organizations to consider alternatives to building their own SOC.

At a Glance: Self-managed SOC

Pros:

- Ideal if you have stringent regulatory compliance requirements and privacy policies

Cons:

- Can be complex and costly to get started
- Difficult to find and retain skilled security staff
- High operational expenses associated with SOC management
- Can take months to achieve operational efficiencies and a baseline maturity

Share the Burden: SOC with a Co-managed SIEM

If building and managing your own SOC is just too overwhelming, that's ok. You have other options. Some organizations prefer to license SIEM technology, but don't want or can't afford to manage it on their own. If you can relate, then you might consider a co-managed SIEM. This is a hybrid approach that involves partnering with a service provider to offload some of the burden.

DON'T FORGET

Here's how a co-managed SIEM works: the organization purchases or leases a SIEM solution, and outsources administration, management, and/or security event monitoring to a third party.

A co-managed SIEM offers flexibility, as your organization can pick and choose the services outsourced versus those kept in house. Typically, the service provider deploys and manages the SIEM 24x7, and you reserve full access to the SIEM console to do your own forensic analysis and investigations.

The pros and cons of a co-managed SIEM

The flexibility of a co-managed SIEM enables you to operate in a more agile manner, procuring or cancelling services when resources fluctuate, or other business factors come into play. For instance, if you lose your security admin, you have the option to outsource additional tasks to your service provider. If a merger increases your staff, you can bring more of that work in house.

Similarly, a co-managed SIEM with optional managed detection and response services provides access to security skills that are in high demand and therefore difficult to obtain. If your organization doesn't have the resources to hire a full-time security analyst or train existing staff, you can benefit from the service provider's expertise. Outsourced staff can be particularly valuable if the service provider has experience with other organizations of the same size.

Organizations that choose to co-manage a SIEM trade some of the cost and complexity of self-management for the cost and effort of managing a service provider relationship. A contract must be negotiated, service levels must be monitored, and terms of engagement must be established.

DON'T FORGET

Outsourcing all SIEM administration, management, and monitoring to a service provider can reduce your operational overhead, but it won't eliminate it. The service provider will still expect you to provide hands-on support and incident response, and you'll need to implement processes to do so effectively.

In addition, it's important to remember that owning a SIEM solution is no different from owning any other IT system. SIEM software requires hardware to run on, and deployment of patches and updates. Licenses must be managed, as well as the vendor relationship. Those responsibilities can't be outsourced. They will continue to reside with the organization.

Finally, it's worth noting that a co-managed SIEM significantly reduces the amount of time it takes to get a SOC up and running. With this approach, you may achieve mature threat detection and response capabilities in a matter of months rather than years.

At a Glance: Co-managed SIEM

Pros:

- Offload the administration and/or management of a SIEM solution to an outsourcer
- Access skilled security personnel
- Spend less than for the DIY option

Cons:

- You remain responsible for managing the cloud-based SIEM and fine-tuning the correlation rules
- It can still take months to achieve operational efficiency and a baseline maturity
- You must manage the service provider relationship

Offload It All: A Managed SOC

If a co-managed SIEM still sounds overwhelming, then you might want to consider a managed SOC, which involves outsourcing the entire SOC to a third-party provider.

Managed SOC providers give you access to the people, processes, and technologies required for a SOC as shown in Figure 5-1, but all of those assets are managed in the provider's datacenter. The data feeds from your networked systems and devices are sent to the provider's SIEM and then analyzed by security experts, who weed out false positives, investigate anomalous behavior, identify actual threats, and help you remediate those threats in real time.

You still need your IT organization and NOC, but now you have access to a fully operational and mature SOC with minimal startup time.

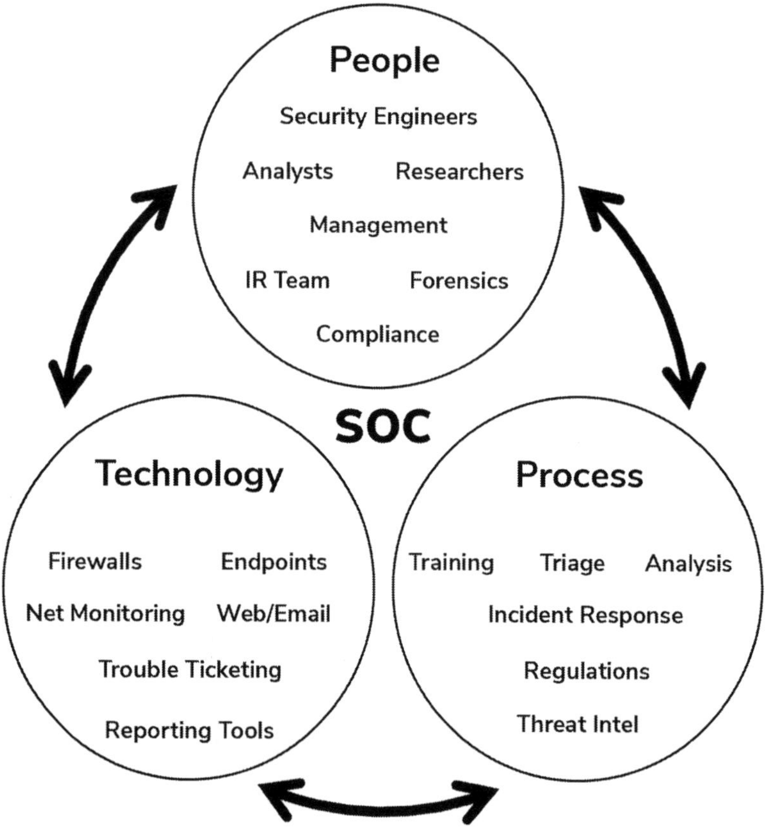

Figure 5-1: A managed SOC provides the necessary people, processes, and technology to reduce the onslaught of alerts to a few prioritized security incidents.

The pros and cons of a managed SOC

A managed SOC offers all the benefits of an on-premises SOC while significantly reducing the cost and complexity involved in building or even co-managing your own.

TIP

A managed SOC provides the following capabilities:

- ☑ Managed detection and response (MDR). MDR is the foundation of a managed SOC. Providers deliver outcome-based services focused on proactive detection of advanced/targeted attacks that bypass your existing perimeter controls. The MDR capabilities are implemented to align with each customer's exact security policies and operational requirements, eliminating the burden of having to determine the best device or method for security monitoring and response.
- ☑ Security expertise. The provider's SOC is staffed with certified security professionals who have a wealth of experience analyzing, investigating, and detecting threats. You also get access to a named security engineer who understands your IT environment and unique business requirements. The security engineer tailors remediation advice to your environment, and provides other recommendations to enhance your security posture.
- ☑ Incident response and crisis support. While you are still responsible for carrying out remediation steps in the managed SOC model, you're not in it alone. Your security engineer prioritizes your incidents and identifies the critical remediation steps your IT team should take. The engineer is available to answer any questions along the way, and after remediation, conducts a post-incident evaluation to determine the effectiveness of your actions.
- ☑ Comprehensive log data collection and retention. A managed SOC provides comprehensive log management that includes data collection, aggregation, and retention. Your log data remains your log data. That means it's stored and organized by the provider in a manner that's easy to access at any time.

☑ Regulatory compliance. Some managed SOCs can help you meet regulatory compliance requirements for HIPAA, FFIEC, GLBA, PCI-DSS, or Sarbanes-Oxley. The security engineer can help you identify and fix security issues to improve your overall security posture and compliance status.

A managed SOC can also help reduce the burden of regulatory compliance by validating your controls, monitoring user behavior, managing security incidents, performing regular vulnerability assessments, and reducing the time and cost involved with preparing for audits.

DON'T FORGET

☑ Predictable monthly pricing. Outsourcing IT or security services to a managed provider usually offers the benefit of a flat monthly fee. This isn't always the case for managed SOC providers, as some may still use a volume-based pricing model, as we discussed in Chapter 3 in relation to SIEM solutions. Ideally, however, the managed SOC provider will not impose a data collection limit, an events-per-second limit, or a limit on availability of your engineer/consultant.

At a Glance: Managed SOC

Pros:

- Provides access to all the capabilities of a mature SOC without the time or effort required to DIY
- Includes assistance with your regulatory compliance efforts
- Significantly reduces the costs required to build and run a SOC

Cons:

- You're still responsible for carrying out remediation steps

Chapter 6

The Role of Managed Services

In this chapter

- Explore outsourcing options for IT and security capabilities
- Learn the difference between MSPs and MSSPs
- Meet a new breed of managed services: the MDR provider

Companies that do not have the resources to hire their own IT and security staff to deploy and manage their network and IT systems can outsource these tasks to a managed services provider (MSP). Though they traditionally cater to small and midsize enterprises, MSPs offer companies of all sizes a convenient way to get the IT and security capabilities they need for a flat monthly rate.

There are a variety of categories of MSPs. For our purposes, this chapter focuses on general MSPs; managed security services providers (MSSPs); and managed detection and response (MDR) services.

Managed Services Providers

A *managed services provider* is a third-party company that delivers IT services to customers on a subscription basis. MSPs typically operate under a service level agreement (SLA), which defines the services as well as the performance and quality metrics that customers can expect as part of their contractual relationship with the MSP.

DON'T FORGET

MSPs typically use remote monitoring and management software to support the customer's IT infrastructure over the network. This software allows the MSP to see what's going on in the customer's IT environment, and remotely troubleshoot and remediate problems as they arise.

What MSPs do

MSPs provide a variety of services, often including:

- ☑ Software installation and support
- ☑ User management, authentication, and single sign-on
- ☑ Account/application provisioning
- ☑ Data backup and recovery
- ☑ Data storage, warehousing, and management
- ☑ Systems management
- ☑ Network monitoring, management, and security
- ☑ Mobile device management

When it comes to security, MSPs are generally responsible for user provisioning and de-provisioning, password resets, remote configuration, and endpoint and perimeter defenses.

What MSPs (typically) don't do

CAUTION

One of the few services MSPs typically don't offer is continuous network and system monitoring for security events. Even if they do provide this service, MSPs tend to lack the in-depth skills to hunt down threats, apply threat intelligence, detect high-priority incidents that require an immediate response, and perform forensic analysis.

Because an MSP does not usually offer them, an IT organization must find a way to procure these additional capabilities. Without 24x7 monitoring, detection, and response, the organization will be challenged to detect unusual or malicious activity in a timely manner.

MSP Advantages and Downsides

Pros:

- Predictable, monthly IT support costs
- Potential cost savings vs. full-time hires
- Access to IT experts
- Faster technology deployment

Cons:

- Loss of control
- Lack of 24x7 security monitoring
- Lack of advanced threat detection and remediation skills

Managed Security Services Providers

Managed security services providers monitor and manage security devices and systems on behalf of their customers. Like MSPs, MSSPs also help companies deploy technology faster and obtain the skills they need through affordable, subscription-based models.

What MSSPs do

DON'T FORGET

At a high level, MSSPs focus primarily on remote device management, vulnerability management, security event monitoring, and alerting. MSSPs configure preventive security controls and provide basic security alerts.

MSSPs may also provide the following capabilities:

- ☑ Off-the-shelf technology for a cloud-based or on-premises SIEM; and, in some cases, a co-managed SIEM owned by the customer
- ☑ Remote device management of security point products like firewalls, intrusion detection/prevention systems, web/email gateways, and Active Directory
- ☑ Managed endpoint protection
- ☑ Remote or onsite incident response provided through a separate retainer
- ☑ Data storage, warehousing, and management

- ☑ Continuous monitoring of network traffic and log management
- ☑ Regulatory compliance reporting

What MSSPs (typically) don't do

CAUTION

MSSPs don't focus on continuous threat detection and response—a must-have for protecting IT environments against advanced threats. Furthermore, MSSPs typically lack the skills required to identify compromised networks and systems, triage advanced threats, or perform forensic analysis. Nor do they provide context for alerting or recommended remediation. As a result, the onus is on the customer to perform triage, analysis, and response. The customer is also expected to have on staff security experts who can determine the validity of alerts and take the appropriate follow-up actions.

When using outsourcing services from an MSSP, it's unlikely you'll pick up the phone and speak to another live human if you have an issue. MSSPs primarily interact with their customers through a service portal and email. Direct communication with security analysts is limited to secondary access via chat functionality and phone.

When it comes to monitoring the IT environment for security threats, MSSPs offer an incomplete solution that can actually cause more problems than it solves. The MSSP doesn't monitor the entire environment, but only specific remote devices, although these are monitored 24x7. This gap in the organization's visibility into its own environment prevents it from effectively monitoring its security posture. As a result, the organization lacks a full understanding of how to best respond to threats.

MSSP Advantages and Downsides

Pros:

- Focus on remote device management
- Basic monitoring and alerting
- Managed endpoint protection via antivirus solutions
- Predictable, monthly IT support costs

Cons:

- Limited knowledge of the customer's IT environment
- Few—if any—security skills for threat triaging and analysis
- Limited network monitoring capabilities
- No dedicated point of contact
- No responsibility for incident response

A New Managed Service: Managed Detection and Response

Managed detection and response services are intended to fill the gap created by MSSPs. While an MSSP looks at ingress and egress traffic, an MDR provider monitors the entire IT environment 24x7, watching traffic as it moves across the network to identify malicious or suspicious activity. MDR providers offer threat detection, incident response, and continuous monitoring—essentially adding up to a cost-effective managed SOC.

TIP

MDR services are ideal for small and midsize businesses with limited investments in security tools and staff; and midsize enterprises that want to supplement their in-house capabilities with outsourced services.

What MDR providers do

Just like the name says, MDR providers focus on threat detection and response. To do so, they must invest heavily in advanced analytics that leverage commodity big data platforms like Hadoop, cloud computing services, and multiple third-party threat intelligence feeds.

MDR providers typically staff their SOCs with highly skilled operators, analysts, and dedicated incident response experts who are responsible for validating potential incidents, gathering the appropriate context, investigating the scope and severity of a threat, and providing actionable advice to the customer. All these functions help customers quickly carry out containment and remediation efforts.

And if you do have a problem? Simply pick up the phone and call your dedicated advisor. Unlike MSSPs, MDR providers communicate directly with the customer via phone or email (rather than a service portal). And you interact each time with the same security professional, who is familiar with your business and your IT environment.

MDR service providers deliver the following:

- ☑ A proprietary technology stack for SIEM, which is included in the service price
- ☑ 24x7 monitoring of events/logs, suspicious activity, and alerts
- ☑ Threat detection, triaging, and forensics analysis
- ☑ Remote incident investigation
- ☑ Recommendations for actionable responses when mitigation/remediation steps must be taken
- ☑ Vulnerability assessments
- ☑ Regulatory compliance reporting
- ☑ Security advisors who serve as extensions of the customer's IT and security teams

What MDR providers (typically) don't do

While MDR providers tend to supply a SIEM, the customer remains responsible for perimeter security controls like firewalls, web gateways, and authentication. That means you'll continue to manage, update, and operate these controls.

MDR providers offer what you might call "lightweight" remote incident response services as part of their core offering. That means you are still responsible for executing remediation and some containment efforts, but you aren't left to your own devices as with an MSSP. MDR providers offer more-descriptive remediation steps and are available to assist you with remediation.

MDR Advantages and Downsides

Pros:

- No need to manage or operate a SIEM on premises
- Focus on threat detection, triaging, and forensic analysis
- Continuous network monitoring
- Actionable intelligence for incident containment and remediation
- A real human to speak to when problems arise
- Access to experienced security staff

Cons:

- No management of perimeter devices, such as firewalls, IDS/IPS, etc.
- Incident response still requires your involvement
- Limited reporting outside of compliance or security-related functions

Caveat Emptor

When it comes to buying a product or procuring a service, most IT organizations know to do their due diligence. It's considered best practice to research providers, evaluate multiple offerings, and verify claims. These practices all help to minimize the risk of making a bad purchase, and they all apply to MDR services.

MDR is a relatively young market, with MSPs and MSSPs as well as pure-play MDR providers vying for position. This being the case, no two MDR providers are the same, and variations across the market can make it difficult to compare service offerings. These variables also reinforce the need to do your due diligence.

When evaluating MDR providers, keep in mind the capabilities that a provider needs to deliver its services. For example, MDR requires expertise in the latest attack vectors, access to global threat intelligence, and advanced technologies to process and filter log data. MSPs and MSSPs must develop these capabilities before they can rightfully claim to provide MDR services.

You can further narrow your list of possible providers by looking for one that specializes in delivering MDR services to organizations of your size, vertical industry, and level of security maturity. Consider a provider with a comprehensive technology stack and the ability to acquire in-depth knowledge of your IT infrastructure.

No new IT service or product comes without some risk. But when selected using due diligence, your MDR provider will reduce your security risk and become a long-term, trusted partner.

Chapter 7

A Closer Look at SOC-as-a-Service

In this chapter

- Explore the capabilities delivered by a SOC-as-a-service solution provider
- Learn how SOC-as-a-service works
- Understand how a SOC-as-a-service solution complements your MSP's services

No security offering does it all. SIEM solutions, MSPs, MSSPs, and MDR providers all have their strengths, but no single one addresses every need. As a result, many organizations find it challenging to put together a complete cybersecurity strategy that provides comprehensive protection against both known and unknown threats.

TIP

However, all is not lost. There's (yet) another category of service providers that specialize in security for companies that can't afford to manage it in house. But there's no need to feel overwhelmed. *Security operations center (SOC)-as-a-service* (SOCaaS) delivers a comprehensive security service with a focus on threat detection and incident response.

This chapter dives into SOCaaS and describes how this solution can improve your security posture by giving you access to must-have people, processes, and technology in a single offering.

SOCaaS: More than MDR

DON'T FORGET

SOC-as-a-service offers more than your traditional managed security services provider. Remember: an MSSP focuses on traditional device management and basic alerting, while SOCaaS is a type of security-as-a-service that's focused on detecting and responding to threats that bypass your preventive controls. When you are looking for security experts who can proactively hunt down threats and give you actionable information to mitigate them, SOCaaS providers are your best choice.

As an outsourced SOC, SOCaaS is more than a managed detection and response solution. It's a turnkey solution focused on real-time threat detection and incident response. SOCaaS solutions also include a cloud-based SIEM, forensic analysis, vulnerability assessment, and compliance reporting. This comprehensive, end-to-end security service is ideal for companies with limited budgets and resources.

Companies that take advantage of SOCaaS essentially outsource the people, processes, and technology needed for a SOC. All of the necessary components and staff of a SOC (SIEM, security analysts, incident responders, etc.) are operated and managed offsite, and delivered as a cloud-based service by the SOCaaS provider. As a result, most of the complexity associated with managing a SOC on premises is eliminated.

With a SOCaaS solution, customers benefit from:

- ☑ Fewer alerts and minimal false positives
- ☑ The ability to leverage existing point products
- ☑ Centralized visibility
- ☑ Security expertise
- ☑ Incident response capabilities
- ☑ Regular vulnerability assessments
- ☑ 24x7 monitoring
- ☑ Predictable operating expenses through a fixed monthly subscription

How SOCaaS Works

SOCaaS is a comprehensive service that leverages a customer's existing infrastructure, the provider's proprietary technology, and the insights and expertise of a dedicated security advisor to deliver a complete security solution.

24x7 network monitoring and log data collection

CAUTION

It's rare to find a company these days that doesn't leverage cloud-based services for one thing or another. Companies today often have a hybrid IT infrastructure that consists of some hardware and applications running on premises as well as some in the public cloud. It's critical that this entire IT environment be monitored 24x7. Otherwise, you will have blind spots where malicious activity can go undetected.

SOCaaS solutions provide the necessary 360-degree visibility into your IT environment. They include a fully integrated monitoring service that can protect IT infrastructure and resources wherever they reside—on the customer's premises, in a public cloud infrastructure, in SaaS applications, or in hosted security services. The SOCaaS provider's security experts have visibility across both cloud and on-premises systems, allowing them to detect attacks wherever they threaten your business. This visibility is achieved in two ways.

Sensors on premises

TIP

A SOCaaS provider uses sensors deployed in specific network segments of the customer's IT environment to inspect network traffic, and to collect network flows and log records from multiple devices, laptops, and servers on those networks. The sensors immediately start gathering system and network activity and send it to the provider's cloud-based SOC, where it's analyzed in real time.

Sensors on premises can be deployed in either an in-line or out-of-band configuration. With an in-line configuration, the sensor can alert and actively block traffic to malicious sources and destinations. In an out-of-band configuration, the sensor can alert and passively monitor (but not block) malicious traffic by listening on a network test access point (TAP) port on a switch.

APIs for cloud services

To monitor cloud activity, SOCaaS providers use virtual sensors that leverage native *application programming interfaces* (APIs) to monitor public cloud infrastructure (like Amazon Web Services and Azure), software-as-a-service applications (like Office 365 and Salesforce), and security-as-a-service environments (like Okta). These APIs provide comprehensive visibility into network, system, and user activity in these cloud environments.

SOCaaS providers can detect the following IaaS events and alerts:

- Suspicious resource usage, such as:
  - Unauthorized access to web console
  - Stop, reboot, terminate instances
  - Massive resource deletions
  - New user and security group creation
  - Updated user profiles
- Malicious activity, such as:
  - Brute-force logins
  - Concurrent access from multiple geolocations
  - Logins from blacklisted IP addresses
  - Suspicious administrative actions

SOCaaS providers can see the following SaaS events and alerts:

- Suspicious activity, such as:
  - Modifications to authentication settings
  - Anomalous sign-in activity
  - Anomalous user account status
  - User password changes and resets
  - Unauthorized geo-based access
- Unauthorized access, as through:
  - Brute-force logins
  - Concurrent access from multiple geolocations
  - Uploading or downloading of sensitive data

Scalable, cloud-based, multi-tenant SIEM

As the "as-a-service" moniker implies, SOCaaS solutions are cloud based. The cloud's highly scalable, multi-tenant architecture plays a critical role in enabling SOCaaS providers to ingest, parse, and analyze unlimited amounts of raw log data from multiple customers.

TECH TALK

A SOCaaS solution combines human and machine intelligence to analyze millions of events in real time for 24x7 threat detection. The machine learning, threat intelligence feeds, and big data security analytics tools collect and correlate security events from all infrastructure, security devices, and applications. This requires a highly scalable environment.

The cloud-based infrastructure allows a SOCaaS solution to perform real-time correlation by:

- ☑ Ingesting billions of events per day
- ☑ Parsing and aggregating log data into structured observations
- ☑ Analyzing data in context using behavior analytics and external threat intelligence feeds to detect advanced malware, emerging network threats, malicious IP addresses, and URLs
- ☑ Prioritizing incidents

The cloud-based environment also allows the SOCaaS provider's security engineers to access security-related data in a variety of forms: raw and structured data, or observations and alerts.

Human-augmented machine learning

Machine learning is playing an increasingly important role in security solutions. It is a field of computer science that involves giving computers the ability to learn and act without being explicitly programmed to do so. The technology makes it easier for organizations to identify advanced cyberattacks but—like a SIEM—it is not the panacea many security professionals hope it is.

Machine learning is not a "set it and forget it" technology. Just as cyberattackers have evolved their threats to bypass preventive controls, they've also morphed their malware and invented new delivery methods to bypass machine learning techniques. That's why SOCaaS providers augment their machine learning technologies with human intelligence.

TIP

Human-augmented machine learning enables SOCaaS providers to detect threats, reduce false positives, and shorten the time between detection and response. The provider's security engineers apply their real-life experience handling emerging threats, which may not be easily characterized by standard machine learning techniques, to identify malicious behavior that bypasses the machine learning technologies.

The expertise you need

A SOCaaS solution's technologies and processes are complemented by skilled security professionals. In addition to the engineers who augment the machine intelligence technologies, the SOCaaS is backed by a team of security researchers who analyze security events on behalf of hundreds of customers and refine the correlation rules used by the SOC. However, each customer also benefits from the personal attention of a named security engineer, who also acts as a trusted advisor for that customer.

This security engineer works with the whole SOCaaS team to monitor your network and analyze your security events for real-time threat detection. When a threat is discovered, the SOCaaS team uses tailored rules and escalations to provide recommended remediation actions.

The SOCaaS staffing model offers customers the benefit of a single point of contact who is intimately familiar with their IT and business operations. Yet, at the same time, the customer doesn't have to worry about hiring and retaining this person, maintaining their skillset, or paying a competitive salary.

In addition to the above, a team of security engineers:

- ☑ Provide ongoing cyberthreat detection in real time
- ☑ Work with each customer to create a customized incident response plan

- ☑ Continually analyze threat intelligence to improve the customer's security controls
- ☑ Conduct frequent vulnerability scans and risk assessments to test security posture

Simplified customer portal

If you'll recall, in Chapter 6 we discussed how outsourcing security to an MSSP can actually limit your visibility into your own IT environment. That's not the case with SOCaaS, whose customers benefit from *increased* visibility, thanks to the use of a simplified customer portal.

The customer portal allows SOCaaS providers to convey pertinent, real-time information to their subscribers about their IT environments. Customers can learn about the security of their networks, applications, and data, and receive actionable security intelligence from their dedicated security engineer. In addition, customized reports enable you to quickly understand your security posture and fulfill compliance requirements.

The simplified customer portal gives you the ability to:

- ☑ Trace the entire lifecycle of a threat
- ☑ Obtain visibility into your own networks
- ☑ Manage regulatory compliance efforts
- ☑ Gauge your security posture at any time using a simple scorecard
- ☑ Receive risk-based remediation advice based on regular vulnerability scans of your environment
- ☑ View outstanding security incidents that need to be addressed

Figure 7-1: A simplified customer portal gives SOCaaS customers visibility into their security posture.

SOC-as-a-Service and Your MSP: A Match Made in Heaven

At the start of this chapter we acknowledged the challenge of piecing together a comprehensive security strategy in light of the various outsourcing offerings available. At this point you may be wondering how SOCaaS fits into the picture. The fact of the matter is SOCaaS and managed services fit together quite nicely.

MSPs deliver a valuable offering by remotely managing IT services and devices to ensure their uptime. If a network issue arises and traffic suddenly slows to a crawl, your MSP can troubleshoot and solve the problem to minimize the impact on your users. However, if that problem proves to be an indicator of compromise, the MSP doesn't have the skills needed to investigate the threat any further. This is where your SOCaaS provider steps in. The SOCaaS provider applies in-depth security skills to hunt down any related threat activity, contain the threat, provide you with remediation advice, and perform forensic analysis.

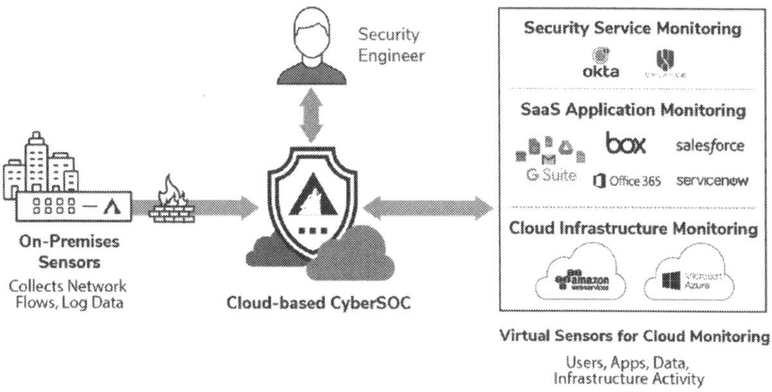

Figure 7-2: A SOCaaS provider delivers 360-degree visibility into and 24x7 security monitoring of your IT environment.

Coming Up for Air

One of the biggest challenges facing SMEs today is managing thousands of security events. More often than not, these companies find themselves drowning in security alerts, unable to make sense of which way is up. SOCaaS solutions offer these organizations an opportunity to come up for air.

The SANS Institute, an information security and cybersecurity training company, evaluated Arctic Wolf Network's SOCaaS solution as an independent third party to determine its suitability for a midsize company. The SANS Institute's lab environment simulated a scaled-down series of systems representing a typical midsize infrastructure. It included a Juniper firewall consisting of a DMZ and an internal interface.

The SANS/Arctic Wolf engagement kicked off with an email from an Arctic Wolf security engineer, who served as SANS' Concierge Security Engineer™ (CSE). The CSE was the single point of contact for all of SANS' SOC-related issues. The CSE helped reduce false positives by vetting incidents to find meaningful and actionable security events and applying context and recommending actions so that SANS knew what to do with the incident.

Setup with the Arctic Wolf service took very little time. SANS connected a sensor to its network, and within minutes, Arctic Wolf confirmed it was seeing traffic and began collecting events.

The SANS Institute accessed a dashboard that provided a high-level status of the environment. Icons allowed SANS to dig deeper to see what was occurring on the network as well as what the CSE was working on. The dashboard provided enough information to allow SANS to investigate something itself or consult the CSE to discuss it further.

SANS evaluated how quickly the Arctic Wolf SOCaaS was able to detect a ransomware event and subsequently send an alert. Instead of using antivirus logs, SANS relied on Arctic Wolf's detection of the event through packet inspection. At 2 a.m., SANS sent Cerber ransomware as an attachment in a phishing email. The ransomware was detonated on a Windows 7 domain workstation. Within seconds, the files on SANS' network shares were encrypted.

Within five minutes of infection, the Arctic Wolf SOC team called SANS to inform them of the infection, providing the IP address of the infected system as well as recommendations for containing the threat.

The SANS evaluation provided insight into Arctic Wolf's monitoring, detecting, and alerting capabilities. SANS concluded that the service allows midsize organizations to get a SOC up and running in minutes and at a fraction of the cost of point solutions or a full-time security engineer.

Source: SANS Review of Arctic Wolf SOC-as-a-Service (https://arcticwolf.com/resources/sans-review-of-arctic-wolfs-soc-as-a-service/)

Chapter 8

Top 10 Next-generation SOCaaS Capabilities

In this chapter

- Review key capabilities you should look for in next-generation SOCaaS solutions
- Learn how a dedicated security engineer can help you improve your overall security posture
- Understand the value of outsourcing your SOC to a SOCaaS provider

Multiple point products and a defense-in-depth strategy no longer suffice in today's cyberspace. To stop advanced persistent threats that bypass preventive controls, IT organizations must have a fully equipped security operations center (SOC) staffed with security experts. When that's not possible, a SOC-as-a-service (SOCaaS) solution is the next best thing.

Important Selection Criteria

CAUTION

The market for SOCaaS solutions is growing rapidly, and actual services can vary. Small and midsize organizations should make sure they get a comprehensive, end-to-end security solution that checks as many boxes as possible. To that end, IT organizations should look for a SOCaaS solution that offers the following 10 capabilities:

- ☑ Vulnerability scanning
- ☑ Continuous network monitoring
- ☑ Log data collection/correlation
- ☑ Cloud monitoring
- ☑ Scalable data architecture
- ☑ Named security engineer
- ☑ Human-assisted machine learning
- ☑ Manual and automated containment
- ☑ Compliance reporting
- ☑ Workflow integration

Vulnerability scanning

The focus of SOCaaS is detection of and response to cyberthreats that evade preventive controls. However, next-generation providers go a step further to help customers proactively strengthen their security posture and reduce the risk of advanced threats.

TIP

This proactivity is achieved with regular vulnerability scans that identify assets at risk. Providers analyze the results of the scan and combine the latest threat intelligence with a deep understanding of a customer's critical assets to develop an accurate, prioritized list of current vulnerabilities. They then provide risk-based remediation advice and recommendations to limit exposure to both known and unknown threats.

Continuous network monitoring

Continuous network monitoring is a prerequisite for detecting malicious activity on the network. Simply watching the network during business hours will not provide the uninterrupted monitoring needed to recognize abnormal activity and reliably detect all threats to which your systems are exposed.

TECH TALK

Along with continuous network monitoring, next-generation SOCaaS providers use a customizable rules engine to define security policies for each customer. This engine allows the provider's security engineers to apply your exact security and operational policies and update them to align with your changing business needs. For example, customized rules can selectively filter out noisy events that represent no real security risk to your environment, or they can help detect known and unknown threats. In this way, a customizable rules engine helps the SOCaaS provider improve efficiency and accuracy when identifying threats in your environment.

Log data collection/correlation

A SOCaaS solution provides comprehensive log management that includes the automatic collection, aggregation, and retention of log data. Data is stored and organized in a secure data architecture, where it can be accessed by the customer at any time.

TIP

Next-generation SOCaaS providers offer unlimited data retention for a specified period with the option to extend it for a fee.

Cloud monitoring

Whether you've fully embraced cloud services or are just beginning to dip your toes in the water, a modern IT environment demands a SOCaaS solution with integrated cloud monitoring. This service will ensure that your entire environment is covered, with no blind spots.

TIP

Look for a service provider that can monitor your IaaS, SaaS, and security-as-a-service solutions. Virtual sensors should be able to use APIs to provide near real-time monitoring of cloud resources and user behavior to ensure they comply with your security policies and are free from threats.

Scalable data architecture

TECH TALK

Look for a SOCaaS provider that leverages a security-optimized data architecture to unify the ingestion, parsing, and analysis of log data, and dynamically scale compute and storage resources based on demand. When complemented by cybersecurity-specific machine learning models, such an architecture can serve as the foundation for security analysts to achieve deep visibility into advanced threats. In addition, the scalable data architecture provides on-demand access to relevant data for incident investigation and is immediately operational with zero setup time.

Named security engineer

Any SOCaaS provider employs skilled personnel necessary to run a SOC. However, when you outsource your SOC to a next-generation provider, you're assigned a security engineer who serves as your single point of contact for all things SOC. Any time an issue comes up, you can turn to the same familiar person who understands your business needs.

DON'T FORGET

One of the many benefits of working with an assigned security engineer is their understanding of your network infrastructure and business risks. Using this knowledge, the security engineer is uniquely positioned to make informed recommendations specifically tailored to your environment. Thus, the security engineer truly becomes an extension of your internal team and a trusted advisor.

A named security engineer:

- ☑ Is a highly skilled analyst responsible for your company's security outcome
- ☑ Conducts daily triage and forensics
- ☑ Customizes services to your needs
- ☑ Reports on the effectiveness of your security posture
- ☑ Provides actionable remediation recommendations that are appropriate for your environment

Human-augmented machine learning

It's humanly impossible to analyze the massive amounts of log data coming from even the most modest IT environments. The only way to efficiently and effectively analyze log data is to utilize machine learning. However, even machine learning isn't foolproof.

CAUTION

Machine learning is great for identifying known threats, but properly categorizing new threat data often requires human expertise. A next-generation SOCaaS provider leverages human expertise to help filter out false positives and fine-tune algorithms as new threats are detected.

Manual and automated containment

Once detected, cyberthreats must be contained to prevent them from spreading further into the environment and to limit their damage. In some cases, containment will require manual effort from your IT staff. However, your dedicated security engineer will provide actionable containment steps and be available to assist you whenever needed.

TIP

There are times, however, when threat containment can be automated. The SOCaaS provider should have automated containment responses set up whenever feasible. This will reduce the burden on you to contain threats, as well as the amount of time it takes to contain the attack, while enabling both teams to focus on remediation procedures.

Compliance reporting

Regulatory compliance is usually a byproduct of good security practices. In fact, regulatory compliance and security have more than half of their policies in common. For example, compliance policies and security both typically address data privacy, log collection, log storage, forensic capability, encryption, firewall zoning, encryption signatures, and network mapping.

TIP

A next-generation SOCaaS provider will offer reporting on these policies and more to help you demonstrate compliance with regulatory requirements. A SOCaaS provider will also help you regularly assess vulnerabilities and reduce the time and cost of preparing for an audit.

Workflow integration

Workflow integration is critical to ensuring that alerts are prioritized and properly escalated for timely remediation. A SOCaaS provider will have onsite workflow integration tools to optimize its own operational efficiencies related to trouble ticketing. Workflow integration that includes your IT staff will help ensure that remediation items are passed on seamlessly from one entity to the other.

The Power of SOC-as-a-Service

CAUTION

There's no doubt that cyberattackers have outpaced the security capabilities of most small and medium enterprises. Attackers know how to bypass perimeter controls, and count on their ability to enter the network undetected and stay there as long as it's financially rewarding to do so. But they won't stop there. As long as there are monetary gains to be had in cyberspace, attackers will be ready to exploit them.

It's time for small and medium enterprises to evolve as well, and seize the opportunity provided by the security industry to improve their security strategies and get a step ahead of cyberattackers.

SOCaaS gives these companies access to the same security capabilities that large enterprises deploy, so they are no longer the easy target. With a SOCaaS solution, you can:

- ☑ Detect and respond to advanced security threats in real time
- ☑ Leverage the expertise of an experienced security staff to improve your overall security posture
- ☑ Work with a named security engineer who understands your IT environment and business risks
- ☑ Reduce the costs associated with protecting your IT environment
- ☑ Focus on the business knowing a trusted provider has your back

As it turns out, cyberthreats *are* the great equalizer.

Case Study: City Improves Security Strategy with SOC-as-a-Service

Your IT organization can do everything right. It can be staffed with functional experts. It can have all the essential security point products in place. And, yet, your company can still be hit with repeated cyberattacks. That was the lesson learned by Nevada's fifth-most populous city when it decided that it was time to strengthen its security efforts.

The city's lean IT team supports administrative offices and public services, including emergency first responders. It's imperative that its IT services maintain their integrity and availability to ensure that the city's organizations can, in turn, respond to residents' needs. Awareness of the security risks to these systems was heightened when the police department experienced a ransomware attack followed by a series of spear phishing attacks. The IT team knew that managing more point products wouldn't enable them to investigate these security issues and respond to them in a timely manner. The organization needed the technology, people, and processes that comprise a SOC.

The city compared the option of building its own SOC to purchasing a comprehensive service from Arctic Wolf Networks. An internal security operations team would offer a better understanding of the city's IT environment and be more responsive. However, 7x24x365 coverage required a team of several people with extensive security expertise and a SIEM, which can be expensive to purchase and maintain. Hiring a team of security analysts, purchasing the software, and then getting everything up and running could take six to 12 moths.

The city opted for Arctic Wolf's AWN CyberSOC because it could be deployed quickly and at far less cost than an in-house SOC. The comprehensive solution eliminates the need to purchase software or hardware. It includes a SIEM managed by seasoned security experts who become an extension of the internal IT team. In addition, the SOC-as-a-Service provides the city with direct access to a Certified Security Engineer™ (CSE).

Within a week of starting the engagement, the city's IT team was notified by AWN of passwords submitted to websites in the clear, as well as phishing attacks on police and fire department personnel. The team also received endpoint mitigation recommendations to quarantine compromised laptops and desktops, removing the guesswork for the IT team.

Today, the Nevada city works hand-in-hand with its AWN CSE, who has become an extension of the internal IT team. The CSE has helped them close up holes in their firewall and even provided the team data and information to fix an issue with their Internet service provider. The CSE is not just there for ransomware and phishing attacks, but also provided them advice on all matters related to cybersecurity.

Glossary

advanced persistent threat (APT): A targeted cyberattack that bypasses preventive controls and leverages multiple attack tactics to obtain network access and remain undetected for long periods of time.

application programming interface (API): Documented commands, functions, and protocols that allow software programs to communicate with each other.

brute-force attack: The process of systematically running through all possible number and/or letter combinations to uncover an account password or PIN.

defense in depth: A security strategy that involves implementing different types and layers of defense mechanisms throughout the IT environment so that if one mechanism fails, the next might stop an attack from progressing further.

departed user access: The unauthorized access of an individual who is no longer working for an organization but still has access to company resources because their accounts were not deprovisioned.

managed detection and response (MDR): A third-party service provider focused on threat detection, incident response, and continuous monitoring.

machine learning: A field of computer science that involves giving computers the ability to learn and act without explicitly being programmed to do so.

managed security services provider (MSSP): A third-party company that monitors and manages security devices and systems on behalf of their customers on a subscription basis.

managed services provider (MSP): A third-party company that delivers IT services to customers on a subscription basis.

mass attack: A cyberattack launched indiscriminately at multiple potential victims rather than at a specific target.

network operations center (NOC): A centralized unit focused on monitoring and managing the enterprise network and the devices on it.

phishing: A cyberattack that leverages social engineering to lure victims into divulging personal or sensitive information.

point product: A technical solution, usually hardware or software, that is designed to address one specific problem.

ransomware: A type of malicious software that encrypts files or data, rendering them illegible, until the user pays a ransom.

security information and event management (SIEM): A system or application consisting of an integrated security information management system and a security events management system. Together they collect and correlate security alerts and events.

security operations center (SOC): A centralized unit comprised of people, processes, and technologies working together to prevent, detect, investigate, and respond to cybersecurity threats and incidents.

security operations center-as-a-service (SOCaaS): A cloud-based, turnkey solution focused on real-time threat detection and cybersecurity incident response.

signature: An identifier based on patterns in code that's associated with malicious activity.

social engineering: The use of deception to trick people into sharing confidential information.

zero-day threat: An attack targeting an unknown vulnerability.